A Bouquet

A token of love.

ALEXANDRA DAY

1996
BLUE LANTERN BOOKS

First printing. Printed in Hong Kong through Colorcraft, Ltd.

Blue Lantern Books
PO Box 4399, Seattle, Washington, 98104-0399

We do not know who first conceived of sending a message by joining the meanings of various flowers together, as words are joined into sentences. We do know that the practice was well established in Turkey in 1717 when Lady Mary Wortley Montague wrote of reading love messages conveyed entirely by means of a package of flowers and gems. She says that one may "send letters of passion, friendship or civility, or even of news, without ever using your fingers." In 1818 a book titled *Le Langage des Fleurs* was published in France, which gave the meanings of each flower, and showed how they could be combined. It was soon translated into English and, as it proved very popular, was followed by many books on the same subject. By the middle of the 19th Century the language of flowers was common household knowledge.

I have long collected Victorian flower scraps. They are so lovely, and their printing so excellent, that I have persistently sought a way to share my collection. In this bouquet I have used them to illustrate a message of loving friendship.

In the back of this book is a list of flower meanings. I have compiled it from the old flower dictionaries that I have. Different listings can have different meanings for a single flower. I have chosen flowers common in the United States, and have preferred the most prevalent definitions.

– Alexandra Day

I send you this bouquet not only for its beauty, but also to send you a message of my regard through the language of flowers.

I send you
Forget-me-nots
in the wish that
our friendship
be always
remembered,

Daisy

and
Daisies,
because of
our many
shared
sympathies
of thought
and
feeling.

Here are Camellias. The white in recognition of your hunger for perfection,

Red

Camellia

the red in
thanks
for the
modesty
of your
excellence.

Fern

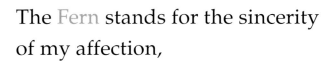

The Fern stands for the sincerity
of my affection,

and the Gloire de Dijon Rose is a messenger of my love.

Gloire de Dijon

Water Lily

I choose the
Water Lily for
your purity of
heart,

and with the
Clematis I praise
the beauty of
your mind.

Clematis

A
Red Poppy
blooms
for the
extravagance
of your
imagination,

Red Poppy

Corn Flowers

and these
Corn Flowers
symbolize
the delicacy
of your spirit.

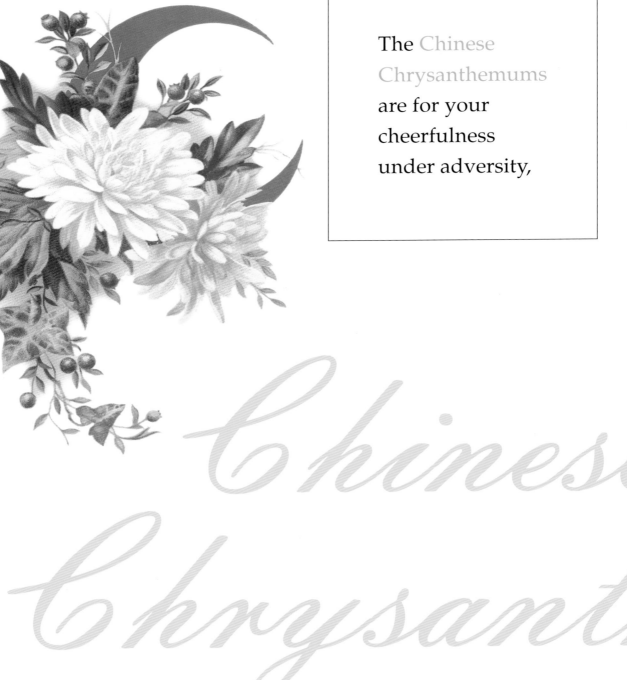

The Chinese Chrysanthemums are for your cheerfulness under adversity,

Chinese Chrysanth

and the Ivy is
here in thanks
for your faithful
friendship.

mum

The Lilac is for the memories that we share,

Lilac

China Rose

and the China Rose for the freshness you bring to every situation.

Geranium

The
Scarlet
Geranium
stands
for the
comfort
friends
offer one
another.

Finally, the Violet asserts the permanance of my affection.

Violet

The Language of Flowers

Acacia : Friendship.

Agrimony : Thankfulness. Gratitude.

Almond, Flowering : Hope.

Alyssum, Sweet : Worth beyond beauty.

Amaryllis : Pride. Splendid beauty.

Anemone, Garden : Forsaken.

Apple Blossom : Preference. Fame speaks him great and good.

Azalea : Temperance.

Bachelor's Buttons : Celibacy.

Basil : Hatred.

Bay Leaf : I change but in death.

Bay Tree : Glory.

Bluebell : Constancy.

Buttercup (Kingcup) : Childishness. Desire for riches.

Butterfly Weed : Let me go.

Cactus : Warmth.

Camellia Japonica, Red : Unpretending excellence.

Camellia Japonica, White : Perfected loveliness.

Camomile : Energy in adversity.

Candytuft, Everflowering : Indifference.

Canterbury Bell : Acknowledgment.

Cardinal Flower : Distinction.

Carnation, Deep Red : Alas! for my poor heart.

Carnation, Striped : Refusal.

Carnation, Yellow : Disdain.

Celandine, Lesser : Joys to come.

Chequered Fritillary : Persecution.

Chickweed : Rendezvous.

China Aster : Variety.

Chinese Chrysanthemum : Cheerfulness under adversity.

Chrysanthemum, Red : I love.

Chrysanthemum, White : Truth.

Chrysanthemum, Yellow : Slighted love.

Clematis : Mental beauty.

Clematis, Evergreen : Poverty.

Clover, Four-Leaved : Be mine.

Clover, Red : Industry.

Clover, White : Think of me.

Columbine : Folly.

Convolvulus : Bonds.

Coreopsis : Always cheerful.

Cowslip : Winning grace.

Crocus : Abuse not.

Crocus, Spring : Youthful gladness.

Crown Imperial : Majesty. Power.

Cyclamen : Diffidence.

Daffodil : Regard.

Dahlia : Instability.

Daisy, Garden : I share your sentiments.

Daisy, Michaelmas : Farewell. Afterthought.

Dandelion : Rustic oracle.

Daphne Odora : Painting the lily.

Dogwood : Durability.

Eglantine (European Sweetbrier) : Poetry. I wound to heal.

Fern : Sincerity.

Forget Me Not : True love. Forget me not.

Foxglove : Insincerity.

Fuchsia, Scarlet : Taste.

Geranium, Ivy : Bridal Favor.

Geranium, Lemon : Unexpected meeting.

Geranium, Oak-leaved : True friendship.

Geranium, Rose-scented : Preference.

Geranium, Scarlet : Comforting. Stupidity.

Geranium, Wild : Steadfast piety.

Goldenrod : Precaution.

Harebell : Submission. Grief.

Heliotrope : Devotion. Faithfulness.

Hellebore : Scandal. Calumny.

Hibiscus : Delicate beauty.

Holly : Foresight.

Hollyhock : Ambition. Fecundity.

Honeysuckle : Generous and devoted affection.

Hyacinth : Sport. Game. Play.

Hydrangea : A boaster. Heartlessness.

Ice plant : Your looks freeze me.

Iris : Message.

Ivy : Fidelity. Marriage.

Jacob's Ladder : Come down.

Jasmine, Cape : Transport of joy. I am too happy.

Jasmine, Carolina : Separation.

Jasmine, Spanish : Sensuality.

Jasmine, Yellow : Grace and elegance.

Lady's Slipper : Capricious beauty.

Lantana : Rigor.

Larkspur : Lightness. Levity.

Lavender : Distrust.

Lilac (Syringa) : Memory.

Lily, White : Purity. Sweetness. Modesty.

Lily, Yellow : Gaiety.

Lily of the Valley : Return of happiness.

Lobelia : Malevolence.

Love in a Mist : Perplexity.

Lupine : Voraciousness. Imagination.

Magnolia : Love of nature.

Mallow : Mildness.

Marigold : Despair. Grief.

Mimosa : Sensitiveness.

Mistletoe : I surmount difficulties.

Morning Glory : Affectation.

Narcissus : Egotism.

Nasturtium : Patriotism.

Nightshade : Truth.

Oleander : Beware.

Orange Flower : Bridal festivities.

Ox Eye : Patience.

Pansy : Thoughts.

Passion Flower : Religious superstition.

Pea, Sweet : Departure.

Peony : Shame. Bashfulness.

Periwinkle, Blue : Early friendship.

Phlox : Unanimity.

Pink, Red : Pure and ardent love.

Pink, Variegated : Refusal.

Pink, White : Ingeniousness. Talent.

Poppy, Red : Consolation.

Poppy, Scarlet : Fantastic extravagance.

Poppy, White : Sleep. My bane.

Primrose : Early youth.

Primrose, Evening : Inconstancy.

Ranunculus : You are radiant with charms.

Rhododendron, Rosebay : Danger.

Rose : Love.

Rose, Bridal : Happy love.

Rose, Burgundy : Unconscious beauty.

Rose, Cabbage : Ambassador of love.

Rose, Carolina : Love is dangerous.

Rose, China : Beauty always new.

Rose, Daily : Thy smile I aspire to.

Rose, Damask : Brilliant complexion.

Rose, Deep Red : Bashful shame.

Rose, Dog : Pleasure and pain.

Rose, Gloire de Dijon : Messenger of Love.

Rose, Hundred-leaved : Pride.

Rose, Multiflora : Grace.

Rose, Mundi : Variety.

Rose, Musk : Capricious beauty.

Rose, Musk (cluster) : Charming.

Rose, Rock : Popular favor.

Rose, White : I am worthy of you.

Rose, White and Red (together) : Unity.

Rose, Yellow : Jealousy.

Rose, York and Lancaster : War.

Rosebud, Moss : Confession of love.

Rosebud, Red : Pure and lovely.

Rosebud, White : Girlhood.

Rosemary : Remembrance.

Snapdragon : Presumption.

Snowball : Bound.

Snowdrop : Hope.

Speedwell : Female fidelity.

Star of Bethlehem : Purity.

Stock : Lasting beauty.

Sunflower, Dwarf : Adoration.

Sunflower, Tall : Haughtiness.

Sweet William : Gallantry.

Thistle, Scotch : Retaliation.

Trumpet Flower : Fame.

Tuberose : Dangerous pleasures.

Tulip : Fame.

Tulip, Red : Declaration of love.

Tulip, Variegated : Beautiful eyes.

Tulip, Yellow : Hopeless love.

Violet, Blue : Faithfulness.

Violet, Yellow : Rural happiness.

Wall-flower : Fidelity in adversity.

Water Lily : Purity of heart.

Witch Hazel : A spell.

Zinnia : Thoughts of absent friends.